Eclectic
Encouragement

Eclectic

Encouragement

Find Hope and Inspiration in the Midst of
Everyday Life

Teresa Alley

ILLUMIFY MEDIA GLOBAL
Littleton, Colorado

Eclectic
Encouragement

Copyright © 2020 by Teresa Alley

All rights reserved. No part of this book may be reproduced in any form or by any means—whether electronic, digital, mechanical, or otherwise—without permission in writing from the publisher, except by a reviewer, who may quote brief passages in a review.

Unless otherwise indicated, Scripture quotations are taken from THE HOLY BIBLE, NEW INTERNATIONAL VERSION®, NIV®. Copyright © 1973, 1978, 1984, 2011 by Biblica, Inc.® All rights reserved worldwide.

Scripture quotations marked ESV are taken from The Holy Bible, English Standard Version®. ESV® Text Edition: 2016. Copyright © 2001 by Crossway, a publishing ministry of Good News Publishers. The ESV® text has been reproduced in cooperation with and by permission of Good News Publishers. Unauthorized reproduction of this publication is prohibited. All rights reserved.

Scripture quotations marked MSG are taken from *THE MESSAGE*, copyright © 1993, 2002, 2018 by Eugene H. Peterson. Used by permission of NavPress. All rights reserved. Represented by Tyndale House Publishers, Inc.

Scripture quotations marked NASB are taken from the NEW AMERICAN STANDARD BIBLE®, Copyright © 1960,1962,1963,1968,1971,1972,1973,1975,1977,1995 by The Lockman Foundation. Used by permission.

Scripture quotations marked NLT are taken from the *Holy Bible*, New Living Translation, copyright © 1996, 2004, 2015 by Tyndale House Foundation. Used by permission of Tyndale House Publishers, Inc., Carol Stream, Illinois 60188. All rights reserved.

The views and opinions expressed in this book are those of the author and do not necessarily reflect the official policy or position of Illumify Media Global.

About the cover artist: While artist Sue Shehan is inspired by all of nature, it is the Colorado skies that captivate her most. Her desire is to capture the viewer's imagination, and to invite them into the vibrant world of pastels.

Published by
Illumify Media Global
www.IllumifyMedia.com
"Write. Publish. Market. *SELL!*"

Library of Congress Control Number: 2020906039

Paperback ISBN: 978-1-949021-70-7
eBook ISBN: 978-1-949021-71-4

Typeset by Art Innovations (http://artinnovations.in/)
Cover design by Debbie Lewis

Printed in the United States of America

Dedication

*I dedicate this book to the unique women of all ages,
whom God has brought into my life over the years. Your
friendship continued encouragement, support,
and wisdom keep my "circle" going!*

*To Tom, my soul mate, husband, and Monday morning
favorite. I love you.*

*To my adult children—Jessie, Amanda, and Mark—
you are my gifts from heaven.*

Contents

Introduction

$\mathcal{I}$ am honored and humbled that you decided this book may be a good read at this time in your life or for someone you care about. Thank you.

My hope is that it may bring you laughter, a bit of pondering, produce a few tears (crying is good for the soul), and convince you what an incredibly special, unique, and loved person you are. I believe with all my heart that women have a precious God-given gift of encouragement. We are relational creatures, and whether introverted or extroverted, there is a desire to show love and encouragement to others. In addition, I hope it inspires and challenges you to keep the Circle of Encouragement going.

1

Coffee Shop Chat And Frogs

Kind words can be short and easy to speak
but their echoes are truly endless.
—Author Unknown

One of the most inspirational ways I receive encouragement is through what I call "latte laughter." As a matter of fact, it was one of the motivators that put my fingers to the keyboard to begin this book.

Women have an incredible way of turning a small wooden table in their favorite coffee shop into a safe haven. In this setting I have been able to share with friends my joys, fears, dreams, and vulnerability. I have made apologies, asked for forgiveness, and shared my brokenness with many table partners. The tears shed and unconditional love given has humbled me more times than I can count.

My precious friend Sue has become my tablemate as of the last few years. Her wisdom and great listening skills have helped me bring many situations into perspective.

Do you realize that it can take a man almost an entire adult lifetime of friendships to achieve this feat? In fairness, I believe it isn't quite as high on their list of emotional needs.

There is so much power in words.

We can speak life and hope into others when the world seems to be crumbling in around them. Yet, in comparison, a few words can bring the final blow of destruction.

Words of authentic encouragement start in the heart: "I am sending him to you for the express purpose that you may know about our circumstances and that he may encourage your hearts (Colossians 4:8). Encouragement is to be mutual. "Therefore encourage one another and build each other up, just as in fact you are doing" (I Thessalonians 5:11).

You may be reading this and thinking, *Easy for some, but I am a person of few words*. I believe these verses pertain to more than just the verbal word.

Most have heard the saying, "Actions speak louder than words." Perhaps your encouragement to others is the affirmation through written words in a short note or special card; maybe you are a prayer warrior for others. You may love to cook and have a gift of meal making for those in need. I recently heard from a neighbor who took an elderly couple from our neighborhood to a doctor appointment, which totaled ninety minutes of driving. Giving of her time was such a special kind of encouragement. Her selfless act reminded me, and more so encouraged me, that I had not visited that elderly couple in weeks. (Confessions of Type A guilt!)

A few years ago a staff member of our then present church told the following story, one of many he had collected over the years:

The Frogs

A group of frogs were traveling through the woods, and two of them fell into a deep pit. All the other frogs gathered around the pit. When they saw how deep the pit was, they told the unfortunate frogs they would never get out. The two frogs ignored the comments and tried to jump up out of the pit.

The other frogs kept telling them to stop, that they were as good as dead. Finally, one of the frogs took heed to what the other frogs were saying and simply gave up. He fell down and died.

The other frog continued to jump as hard as he could. Once again, the crowd of frogs yelled at him to stop the pain and suffering and just die. He jumped even harder and finally made it out. When he got out, the other frogs asked him, "Why did you continue jumping? Didn't you hear us? The frog explained to them that he was deaf. He thought they were encouraging him the entire time.

What encourages you? What do you glean from encouraging others? What do you need from encouragement? Write it. Speak it. Act it out! It can lift you up on a hopeless day, spread light through your dark place, and replace restlessness with contentment.

Soul Food

"Pleasant words are a honeycomb, sweet to the soul
and healing to the bones."

(PROVERBS 16:24 NASB)

Personal Reflection Or Group Discussion

1. Read Colossians 4:8: "I am sending him to you for
    the express purpose that you may know about our
    circumstances and that he may encourage your hearts."
    What has been a meaningful example of ways you have
    been encouraged by others?

2. Is vulnerability something you find comfortable or
    challenging? Why or why not?

3. Share an activity that gives you inspiration and why.

Journal, Doodle, Reflect

2

Master Tailor and the Wannabe Seamstress

"Tapestry"

My life is but a weaving, between my God and me.
I do not choose the colors, He worketh steadily.

Ofttimes He weaveth sorrow, and I in foolish pride,
forgets He sees the upper, and I the underside.

Not till the loom is silent and the shuttles cease to fly,
will God unroll the Canvas and explain the reason why.

The dark threads are as needful in the skillful Weaver's hand,
as the thread of gold and silver in the pattern He has planned.
—*Author unknown*

*M*y mother was an accomplished seamstress. She made clothes for herself as well as for my sister and me. Additional items included clothes for our baby dolls, prom dresses, and even suits for my stepfather in their early years of marriage.

I made worthy attempts at the sewing machine starting in seventh grade home economics class. I did complete a few outfits, but mostly because of the encouragement from my mom and the sweet, gray-haired home economics teacher, Mrs. Finch.

What I remember most about the class was the frustration of turning the garment inside out and ripping threads that continually seemed to find their way into the wrong places. I can still see the white handled seam ripper I used. But Mrs. Finch taught me that those misplaced, unwanted threads were a necessary part of the creation. They were a learning experience of patience and perseverance with a beautiful, completed outcome.

I believe we focus too often on those dark threads— the "underside" of the weave. To some it may look like fear, hauntings of the past, guilt, shame, or perhaps the never-ending unfulfilled expectations of everyday life.

In her daily devotional, *Jesus Calling*, Sarah Young writes, "You inhabit a fallen, disjointed world, where things are constantly unraveling around the edges."

I felt that unraveling at one point in my life. It took me a long time to let go of the chains that held me from the freedom of God's grace. I looked at myself as unworthy and not deserving of that grace. I lost sight of my "upper side." I knew He loved me and I loved Him, but it wasn't until I learned to love Him with all of me—even my underside—that I came to understand His forgiveness and unconditional love.

Whether it is the upper side or underside of your weave, all the unique parts of you are shared with the Creator. It may be somewhere so deep within the threads of your life that it feels lost. Perhaps it has darkened, a bit rough around the edges from lack of exposure. Maybe it feels almost nonexistent.

Start now, this day, acknowledging, accepting and loving yourself just as you are. Trust the One who created you in His image, a beautiful Canvas woven by the Master Tailor.

Soul Food

"For you created my inmost being; you knit me together in my mother's womb. I praise you because I am fearfully and wonderfully made; your works are wonderful, I know that full well. My frame was not hidden from you when I was made in the secret place, when I was woven together in the depths of the earth. Your eyes saw my unformed body."

(PSALM 139:13-16)

Personal Reflection Or Group Discussion

1. The author refers to a time she felt her life unraveling. Are you presently or have you in the past found yourself in a similar situation? Explain.

2. Assuming you have had this experience, list some adjectives that describe how you felt going through this period of unraveling. Give additional adjectives that describe your feelings once you were "out on the other side" of this situation.

3. If you could describe your life as a tapestry, what would it look like?

Journal, Doodle, Reflect

3

Out on a Limb

What one regards as interruptions are precisely one's life.
—*C.S. Lewis*

When you hear the word *trust*, what comes to mind? Reliance on another, assured hope, or having faith in someone or something?

Maybe the word invokes a feeling that would appear to be the very opposite of the word itself—doubt, suspicion, fear, or even risk.

Picture in your mind an inexperienced tree-climbing kitten that manages to get herself stuck high upon a tree limb. Frozen with fear, trusting no one, she remains set in place until her rescuer cradles her back to safety.

Trust is a small, five-letter word, yet it carries a lot of weight. From the time we are born, we have a need and a necessity to put trust in those who are caring for us. That trust and dependency continues throughout our childhood, teenage years, and obviously lessens as we reach the stage of young adults. Unfortunately, for many, the trust is broken before we reach the stage of our own independence, leaving confusion, heartache and a multitude of scars.

When I was a young girl, I came to the conclusion that trusting and risk-taking come hand in hand. In a non-elective manner of having to grow up fast, I grappled with a number of issues.

In my struggles my mother sent me to a recommended counselor, a kind man with a salt-and-pepper beard. Though we only had a few sessions, the discussions led to some very poignant questions on his part. I remember being hesitant and a bit fearful answering truthfully.

In our last session I specifically remember that his advice, although caring, was not as helpful as I had hoped it would be. He suggested that I find ways to manage my feelings, yet offered me no specific tools to accomplish this. Some of the situations in my life were beyond my power to change, so I was hard-pressed to find helpful ways to handle my emotions.

Still, it was all he gave me, so I set out to try to "handle" circumstances that I felt were uncomfortable or even betrayals of my trust. I would and could do whatever was necessary to keep myself emotionally strong and emotionally untouchable. It became a constant process of leaning into my own strength. But little did I know what an exhausting experience that can be.

In Matthew 14:22–32 the apostle Peter's amazing example of faith and trust provides a lesson for us all. After Jesus performed the miracle of multiplying five loaves of bread and two fish to feed over 5,000 on the shores of Galilee, He sent the disciples ahead of Him, across the lake. The boat had drifted out about three miles, as there were strong winds during the night.

Around four a.m. Jesus came walking out on the water toward them. Their reaction: "It's a ghost!" Jesus reassured them, "It is I, don't be afraid."

Interestingly, Peter was the only one who reacted in faith: "Lord, if it's you, tell me to come to you on the water."

Jesus told him to come.

Peter proceeded out of the boat, walked toward Jesus, but in the process looked down at the tumultuous waves and started to sink, crying out, "Master, save me!"

Jesus didn't hesitate. He reached down, grabbed Peter's hand, and said, "Faintheart, what got into you?"

When he took his eyes off Jesus and focused on the high waves, his faith wavered and he plummeted!

I continued into my early twenties with an attitude that living risk-free, when it came to relationships, was uncomplicated and didn't mess with my heart. I worked as a flight attendant with a major airline, and my home base was in Denver, Colorado. One evening something happened that caused an interruption to my impenetrable plan. While sitting on a reserve shift, I was called to work a red-eye flight. After finishing our service and cleanup, most passengers were beginning to doze off. Perfect time to get engrossed in my current read. Little did I know that God had an entirely different agenda for the remainder of the flight.

My coworker, Ron, joined me on the jump seat and began a conversation. He was a talker, so there was no stopping

him. He began sharing some very interesting facts about his
background, as well as how the Lord had brought him to this
present job. I became fascinated and after several minutes
closed my book and placed it upon my lap for the remainder
of the flight.

Ron was very open about his past, and some of it was a bit
dark. He didn't hesitate to give God the glory in the positive
changes that had occurred as he continued to put full trust in
the Lord's plan for his life.

Full trust, really? Wasn't that a bit risky? I believed in God.
I had accepted Jesus Christ as my Savior when I was twelve. I
admit, my walk with God looked more like me in the lead,
glancing back occasionally to see if He was "following." This
"full trust, Lord of my life" concept was a new thing.

As I sat there contemplating Ron's words, I gazed at the
overhead bins above the sleeping passengers. Whenever I had
a serious issue in my life and exhausted all other avenues, I
would "take God down off the shelf" (or the overhead bin in
this case!) and call upon Him.

I had trusted in myself first and never allowed Him the
trust to show me what His power, grace, and unconditional
love could do with my life. I wanted that. I wanted all of it.
The Holy Spirit was on the move, and I recommitted my life
to Christ that night. That happened forty years ago and it still
brings such joy to my heart reliving the memory.

The trust started slowly, and I can honestly say it was
sometimes scary. Do I waver and take my eyes off Jesus as Peter
did? You bet—*many* times. Is my life risk-free, as I had desired
earlier in my life? No way! The trust has grown with each new

season of life God has allowed me to be a part of. He continues to be ever faithful. I am forever grateful that God put me on that two a.m. check-in for the flight that changed my life.

Holding onto His hand, begin today, slowly making your way out on the limb. If you waver and fall, which you will, He is faithful and will always catch you!

Soul Food

"In this world you will have trouble. But take heart! I have overcome the world."

(JOHN 16:33)

Personal Reflection Or Group Discussion

1. Is your view of trust different now as an adult than when you were growing up? If yes, how?

2. Read Matthew 14:22–32. Picture yourself upon the boat as one of the disciples. Remember Jesus sent you out ahead of Him across the lake. The boat has drifted about three miles, and the winds are growing stronger. It's four a.m. and dark! Eerily, a figure appears several yards out walking on the water toward the boat. As the figure comes closer he speaks the words, "It is I, don't be afraid." What might have

been your honest reaction? Would you have attempted the "water walk"? Discuss how wavering and taking our eyes off Jesus can cause us to sink.

3. Share your experience of being "out on a limb" and how you trusted Christ to bring you to a safe place. How was this a game changer in your relationship with Him?

Journal, Doodle, Reflect

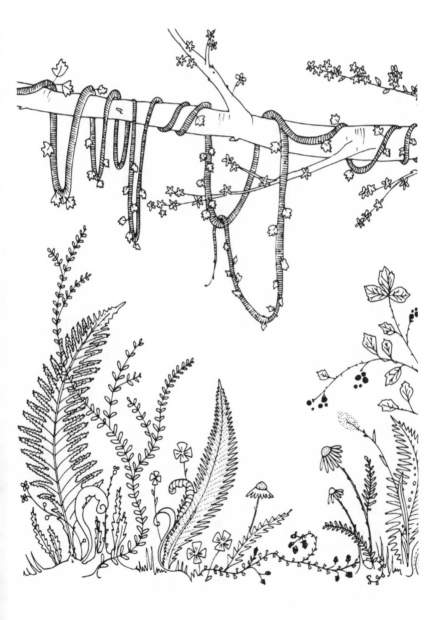

4

Sunrise, Security, and Sea Shells

Nothing can dim the Light which shines from within.
—MOPS Newsletter, February 2015

Mexico is one of my favorite places to spend time, especially along the Sea of Cortez in San Jose del Cabo. I am in awe of (even a bit fearful) the ocean due to its vastness and power. There are so many amazing creatures that call it home, whether they live within its depth or along the shore. I am never bored with the sound of the waves crashing or that first rush of cold salt water that hits my legs on my daily walk. The early morning sunrise upon the horizon has its own dimension of beauty. The light that spills across the waves creates colors of orange, pink, and yellow in the sky. It is my glimpse of heaven. I continually give thanks to my Creator, who has given me the privilege to view it all.

Several years ago, some dear friends invited us to join them in ownership of their beautiful home in San Jose. We were honored and thrilled at the opportunity. As I noted earlier, I love this area in Mexico; this specific beach is tranquil, and the sand feels like powder beneath your feet.

One particular morning I made my way west along the shore. I had such a strong sense of God's presence and was filled with anticipation. I came upon the familiar large grouping of multicolored rocks, which begin on the shore and gradually gather height making their way about fifteen to twenty yards out into the ocean. This is a popular place for the local fishermen. It is common sight, right after sunrise, to see several pangas anchored in the sand while the men toss their nets out into the water.

I tentatively placed myself upon one large rock, careful not to disturb the birds perched and focused on catching their morning breakfast. I became more observant of this small environment before me. There were four different species of birds aligning the rocks—pelicans, seagulls, cranes, and one lonesome brown-and-gray feathered sandpiper scuttling along the shore. Not to mention the hundreds of black crabs, which are camouflaged among the rocks. The pelicans, largest of all the birds, sat on the highest groups of rocks next to the ocean. A definite viewpoint advantage! The seagulls were in close second, and the cranes had a bit of advantage with size and speed if they were thinking ahead! But the most interesting was the lone little sandpiper scuttling along the shoreline. He couldn't seem to decide if the shore, the water, or the mountain of rock would be the best perch. They each seem to know their place of simple survival secured within the hierarchy of groupings. My thoughts turned to how we humans so easily divide ourselves among the comfort zones we have come to know and think to be safe. We have a netting of false security, hiding imperfections that we think make us unacceptable to others. I know I have allowed myself to fall into that form of deception way too often over the years.

Leaving my feathered friends behind, I headed back toward the villa, collecting seashells as I went. The day before had brought massive waves onto the shore, so I had many shells to choose from. Halfway down the beach I realized I was trying so hard to look for the perfect shells, those that hadn't been marred by the pounding ocean waves against the rocks and shore. Many had cracked edges and were dull in color and definitely not considered pretty to the human eye. And then the thought hit me. I am like these shells: washed up on the shore, imperfect, chipped around the edges and sometimes broken, and bleached by the elements of life. I'm not filled with sand (thank goodness) but the gift of the Holy Spirit. God never expects perfection; He sees me as a whole person. He can easily mend the cracks, shine up the exterior, and clean me up from the inside out. I am forever grateful.

P.S. I am adding these less-than-perfect shells to my "perfect" collection!

Soul Food

"Even though on the outside it often looks like things are falling apart on us, on the inside, where God is making new life, not a day goes by without his unfolding grace."

(2 CORINTHIANS 4:17 MSG)

Personal Reflection Or Group Discussion

1. If you could identify yourself with one of the four groups of birds described on the beach (pelicans, seagulls, cranes, and sandpipers) which would it be and why?

2. What are your thoughts regarding the author's observation of how people may place themselves in certain comfort zones?

3. Share your "glimpse of heaven."

Journal, Doodle, Reflect

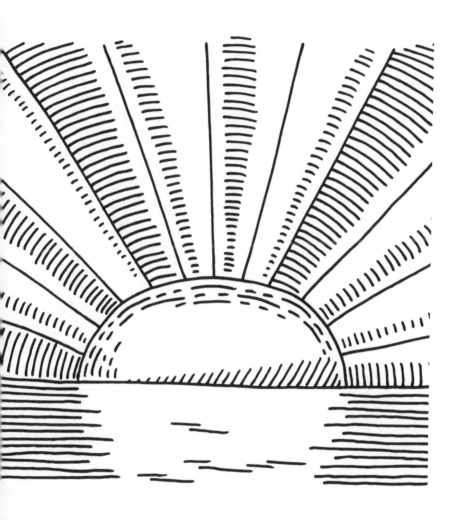

5

Sunrise on the Sea of Cortez

My morning awakens to the crashing of waves
onto the pre-dawn shadowed sand.

There is a peaceful stillness along the beach.
Even the chattering of the Gray Wren is silent.

The soft cool sand cushions my feet as I make my way
along to my favorite viewing sight.

At water's edge, I join a group of pelicans
perched upon the rocks.
Their focus is "breakfast" swimming below.

A cool breeze stirs against my skin
as I eagerly await in anticipation.

A painted splash of pink floods the horizon,
filling in the expanse between ocean and sky.

The sun emerges and the waves take on a glittering brilliance
like jewels dancing across the water.
Don't look away!

Within minutes, the magnificent ball of fire,
fully risen has colored the sky.
I am enveloped in the welcoming warmth it provides.

The birdsong of many begin greeting the day.
In harmony and thankfulness, I bask in the glory
of His wondrous creation.
—Teresa Alley

Soul Food

"And God said, "Let the water under the sky be gathered to one place, and let dry ground appear." And it was so. God called the dry ground "land," and the gathered waters he called "seas." And God saw that it was good."

(GENESIS 1:9-10)

Personal Reflection Or Group Discussion

1. Most of us, when asked, have a "happy place." It may be outside our home state, the town we live, in or right in our own home. It can bring a variety of feelings and emotions. What is your happy place and why?

2. What colorful adjectives describe how you feel and what you see when you are in this special place?

3. Who would you invite into this space?

6

Just a Clay Pot?

Unglazed,
battered and fractured—but not broken
muddied in color,
bare and unadorned,
void, perishable.
—Teresa Alley

Depression is something I have dealt with most of my adult life. There are a number of things, which have triggered the depression—hormonal, emotional, or situational. Life can bring joy but can also deplete us in many ways. In those discouraging times the logical part of me thought, *Snap out of it. Get a grip.* But usually the dark cloud of depression felt too heavy, encompassing my whole being. Sometimes it felt as if I was in a slow-motion maelstrom, with no strength to bring myself to the surface and break away. My life view was very different in those periods. Normally a social and extroverted

person, I avoided group events and would sometimes cancel
commitments that usually brought fullness to my life. My
immediate family members knew of this ongoing struggle
and tried their best to be loving and encouraging. I struggled
with feelings of aloneness. I felt separated from the Lord and
unworthy. I saw my identity through the looking glass of the
enemy.

I had but two choices: turn away in bitterness and anger
or ask for help. My reprieve would come when I finally fell
to my knees and literally cried out to God. I confessed that I
could no longer handle the situation on my own. I asked the
Lord to show me His perspective and not the clouded view of
the enemy. Over time, through much prayer and journaling,
this was what God's Spirit conveyed through my writing:
"Though I have had brokenness and despair as companions,
His healing touch continues. Though I have felt spiritually void,
His Spirit continues to live in me. The path of loneliness may
seem endless, yet He has never left my side. When darkening
thoughts become a stronghold, I need only to ask and His
Light overpowers the darkness. He is my Constant."

No more shame or denial. In my relinquishment to
Christ, I came to a better understanding of His unconditional
love as well as seeing myself through His eyes. Created in His
image, though I may have a few cracks here and there (okay,
more than a few), it only better shows His light from within.
My willingness to trust in His will, instead of my own, provides
a great sense of freedom. He is my Help and Protector, my
Constant. As Christ shares with us in John 15, we have to
learn to live in Him as He lives in us. We can't really live a

fruitful life unless we are joined to Him. Joy comes from being in a consistent relationship with Him, in the good times and not so good times. I gratefully accepted my identity through Him. Did the depression leave me? No, not entirely. Is it part of my identity? Not anymore! But I have come to have an acceptance of it in a much different way. I am able to openly share with others without embarrassment. The added bonus is vulnerability and empathy toward others who have the same struggle.

Soul Food

"If you only look at us, you might well miss the brightness. We carry this precious Message around in the unadorned clay pots of our ordinary lives."

(2 CORINTHIANS 4:7 MSG)

Personal Reflection Or Group Discussion

Author's note: I wavered in writing this chapter, as it may be viewed as less than encouraging. A large part of my book is focused on my willingness to be vulnerable and bring encouragement to others, and say, "You are not alone!" There are some who have the opinion depression is a weakness, not real or a darker part of something else. Unfortunately, this has kept some people hiding in shame and denial, not getting the help they need. Depression can be a difficult and painful subject for many, bringing a handful of other issues along with it. If you are discussing this book in a group setting, please be prayerfully mindful of others who are personally experiencing depression (or have loved ones going through depression). "You can't understand someone until you've walked a mile in their shoes." The person who first uttered these profound words is lost to history, but the importance of empathy toward others still remains strong.

1. Have you experienced a time in your life when you had an event similar to the author's description of crying out to God and confessing the need for His help? If comfortable, describe that process.

2. Joy is one fruit of the Holy Spirit, but depression can zap the joy right out of our lives! Read John 15:4, 9, 11. From a personal standpoint, share your thoughts on these verses.

3. How can satan (I refuse to capitalize his name) use this on his attack against our relationship with Christ? What can we do to combat this?

Journal, Doodle, Reflect

7

He Has the Whole World
in His Hands

"Hope" is the thing with feathers,
That perches in the soul,
And sings the time without the words,
And never stops at all.
—Emily Dickinson,
"Hope Is the Thing with Feathers"

Legends say that hummingbirds float free of time, carrying our hopes for love, joy, and celebration. The hummingbird's delicate grace reminds us that life is rich and beauty is everywhere. Every personal connection has meaning, and laughter is life's sweetest creation.

Did you know that hummingbirds have a maximum forward speed of 30 mph and 60 mph in a dive flight! Their species is the smallest bird in the world. (The bee hummingbird is only 2.25 inches long!) During migration some species fly

500 miles nonstop across the Gulf of Mexico. They can't walk or hop. They scoot sideways using their feet while perched. Their heart rate is more than 1200 beats per minute. The average human heart beats 60–100 per minute.

I held a humming bird in the palm of my hand today. It is early September and a beautiful Colorado afternoon. I am sitting on my patio enjoying the warmth of the sun, waiting for my son Mark to arrive. He recently has moved to an apartment in downtown Denver, and truthfully, I think he knows these visits mean the world to me as I adjust to his absence from our home for the second time in his life.

If I had been moving about the patio immersed in my weekly cleaning frenzy, I would have missed one of the most amazing and tender moments of my life. My devotion that morning had been on the subject of resting in the Lord, giving my mind a break, and giving over control of my life to Him. What better way to continue the devotion by enjoying the warmth of His creation, the stillness of the day, and sitting in His presence.

It was then I heard the light thud behind me. Within seconds my ears processed the squawking of a precious little humming bird. He had flown into our large picture window and fallen upon (thankfully) the wicker rocker, which sat below. As I approached, he quieted. Lying upon his belly with wings spread out his eyes wide open, it was obvious he was in shock and possibly in pain. I waited a few minutes, observing him, deciding he may only have bit of life left. Gently, I scooped him up in my right hand. In my humanness, I thought I could bring him some sort of comfort in those last fleeting moments.

Surprisingly, he remained conscious and slowly came to a calmer state. He was virtually weightless in my hand; I could only feel his tiny talons upon my skin. He was beautifully colored, delicate, and so vulnerable. I had never seen a humming bird up close without it being in rapid movement. I was in awe! I was actually able to stroke his tiny head with my index finger.

God then chose to give me an aha moment—something He graciously does from time to time. I felt the Lord conveying His message of hope: *Teresa, my dear child, I know there are certain times of your life you are so broken and in need of My direction. You just need to be held. I promise to comfort you and calm you and protect you from all harm. I gaze upon you as my beautiful, amazing, and vulnerable creation. I hold you in the palm of My hand. I see you where you are. I hear your whispers of shame and pleas of forgiveness. I feel your brokenness, heavy heart, and fears. I will never leave you nor forsake you.*

Ever so gently I released the little humming bird upon the nearby lilac bushes, where it soon took flight onto its next destination, "floating free of time, carrying our (my) hopes for love, joy, and celebration." Next time you see a humming bird, celebrate the love and joy God has for you!

Soul Food

"So do not fear, for I am with you; do not be dismayed,
for I am your God. I will strengthen you and help you;
I will up hold you with my righteous right hand."

(ISAIAH 41:10)

Personal Reflection Or Group Discussion

1. The author described a personal aha moment with the Lord. Share one of your most recent aha moments.

2. Resting in the Lord does not always come easy, as our everyday life can be so distracting. Compare some of the ways you have had challenges/successes with this practice.

3. Close you eyes and take a long, slow breath. Visualize God holding you. What does it look like? How do you picture God? How do you see yourself? What emotions do you feel?

Journal, Doodle, Reflect

8

Daddies, Daughters, and Treasures

Remember, no effort that we make to attain something
beautiful is ever lost. Somewhere, sometime, somehow, we
shall find that which we seek.
—Helen Keller

MEMORY BOOKMARK: Living on a wheat ranch with only one other house on the same property within several miles brought a different kind of loneliness for the little girl. The other family also had a girl close in age, and when schedules coincided it was a special time.

There was an old gray barn on the property, which was home to a black-and-white Shetland pony named Missy and two other horses owned by her parents. For her the barn was a place of adventure. She loved the earthy smell when she entered the barn: the horses, hay, and dust that accumulated over the years activated her senses and instilled joyful memories. Small rays of sunshine would filter through cracks in the walls and roof, bringing through just enough light for her to not be afraid. Her father was an expert handler of horses; it was one of his passions. She would often sit and watch while he trained horses in the corral outside the barn. There were times she sat in the saddle alongside her dad. She was so afraid of those beautiful, big beasts, yet she desperately wanted to ride one like her daddy. If he could have just been more patient with her fears, if they would have had more time, maybe it could have become a passion for her too.

Exploring the barn brought forth old rusty horseshoes, feathers, and small farm gadgets that were no longer useful. But it was up on the hayloft where her treasure lay. Each visit, she would climb up the small man-made ladder attached to the barn wall to reach the loft. There, next to where the barn wall of two-by-fours and the floor of the loft adjoined, lay a perfectly constructed nest made of hay and twigs. Within that nest lay a long abandoned bird egg. She would hold it gently in her small hands, admiring its faded blue color and the smooth exterior. To the seven-year-old, it was a mystery. What kind of bird could this belong to? Where was the mommy bird? She felt so lucky to call this treasure hers. Each time she carefully replaced it, with anticipation of the egg hatching upon her next visit.

MIXED MEMORIES: Late summer was the busiest season on the ranch. The large wheat harvesting combine machines were a common sight. It was also an exciting time when, on a rare day, she was allowed to ride with her daddy. With her snack bag of Oreo cookies, she was hoisted up to her father's arms and set on the platform. Next to him, she felt such a sense of protection. If he could handle this big, green machine, he could do anything! He drove the lines so straight, making the turns at the precise times, the blowing dust slowly layering upon his face and arms. Did he know how much she wanted him to notice her noticing him?

SCATTERED MEMORIES: She opened the Christmas gift with longing excitement. The shape of the box had given it away. It was a special doll she had spied at a local store while shopping with her mom. Blond hair, blue-eyed Chatty Cathy. The little girl knew that a pull of a string on the back of the doll's neck would bring forth all kinds of cheerful conversation. She thought, *Oh, a wonderful new friend, someone who will be there to share each day with me.*

Because of the loud noise of the combine, conversation was nearly impossible. But she would imagine that if not for that, her daddy would have shared stories about when he was her age, maybe even what kind of adventures he might have had. Perhaps when the job is done and they head back to their house, they would have their talk. In the innocent ways of a young child, she remained hopeful and content with those thoughts.

The pull string didn't work on the Chatty Cathy doll. The sound that came was scratchy, like a slightly broken record. Even though it brought tears to her eyes, she loved the doll anyway. The day after Christmas her daddy made an exchange for another doll. She waited patiently until he returned that afternoon. So overwhelmed, as he handed it over, she hugged his legs in thankfulness. She was oddly aware he did not return the hug.

It was their playtime. He was in a happy place. He lay flat on his back on the family room floor, with his arms above his head, and coaxed the little girl to step onto his hands. Bringing his feet up to where she could hold them for stability, he slowly raised her up in the air. She felt on top of the world! He held her still until she could comfortably let go of his feet, balancing on her own. Slow and steady, up and down she moved. He smiled as he told her how well she was doing. *This was what daddies and daughters are supposed do*, she thought.

This story does not have a sad ending, as one might imagine. Over the years, with times of unreturned hugs, of promises made and never fulfilled, when her anger raged and her heart hardened, when she tried to forgive and forget, God felt her every emotion and grieved with her. She cried out to God and He heard her cries. He reached down from on high and took hold of her; He drew her out of deep waters. He became her Deliverer, her Rock, the One in whom she could take refuge (Psalm 18). She heard Him whisper, "I rejoiced the day you called me Abba Father and came to the realization you are the daughter of the One True King."

She watched from her kitchen as her husband wrestled with their two young daughters on the family room floor. The small amount of sadness, which still remained in her heart, was covered by the joy of the scene before her. It was a reminder of thankfulness for this amazing man God so perfectly placed in her life. He is the visual—in the flesh—of a father who will hug and hold hands, wipe tears, guide with love and wisdom, and continue to remind his children they are God's treasure.

Soul Food

"But you are a chosen people, a royal priesthood, a holy nation, a people belonging to God, that you may declare praises of him who called you out of darkness into his wonderful light."

(I PETER 2:9)

Personal Reflection Or Group Discussion

1. Beginning with Genesis 1 the first family unit was made. Created in His image, it was a good thing. Along with this came free choice, and so began the saga of humanity's good and not-so-good choices in our family units. The author shared some childhood memories with her father, which caused some sadness and longing for more. As her relationship with the Lord grew, so did her understanding of her father. (See poem "I'll Do It My Way" in the following chapter.) If comfortable, share the importance of your life experience being a daughter to your father. And, if applicable, share your perception of your daughter and her relationship to her father.

2. As a noun, treasure means a "very valuable object." Used as a verb, it means to "keep carefully or value highly", possibly as a memory. As a child, what do you recall you considered

your treasure? From your present adult perspective, why do you think this item was so special?

3. We are so blessed to have a Creator who is truly the best Father one could ever imagine. No matter where we've been or what we've done, He waits with open arms of unconditional love. Share your thoughts as to why the author chose the quote by Helen Keller at the beginning of this chapter.

Journal, Doodle, Reflect

9

I'll Do It My Way

Always curious of your childhood, only parts
you chose to share.
But looking into my grandparent's eyes, I knew
how much they cared.

They had their private turmoil; did it cause
your heart to ache?
Deceit, false fronts, confusion, did it
push you to escape?

Perhaps that's when the prideful independence
took its stay.
Your mantra moving forward with the words,
I'll do it my way.

Dad, I'm sorry for your childhood pain and
the innocence you lost.

Forced to grow up much too quickly seeking wisdom
from other gods.

You met her as a youth and she became the
Apple of Your Eye.
Was there a new sense of security when she
became your bride?

Naval Service, then the wheat fields—Horse Heaven Hills
your place to roam.
Your strong and hardworking spirit had found
its way back home.

Next came fatherhood, as I arrived,
on a cold December day.
I'd take bets, as whiskey shots were passed,
you said, "I did it my way!"

Sometime later, a precious bundle was sent
from Heaven above.
God knew I would need this beautiful blonde
to share in sisterly love.

With love, I say my final goodbyes, where you chose
your ashes to lay.
I imagine you looking upon with those familiar words,
"They did it my way!"
—Teresa Alley

Soul Food

"Trust GOD from the bottom of your heart; don't try to figure out everything on your own. Listen for GOD's voice in everything you do, everywhere you go; he's the one who will keep you on track."

(PROVERBS 3:5 MSG)

Personal Reflection Or Group Discussion

I am sure we can all agree with the statement: *There are no perfect parents!* Sometimes we can be quick to impose judgment on our parents for our character flaws or negative state of affairs. It is easy to forget they, too, once had parents who may have set the generational flaws in motion. It can all come down to a famous quote popularized by US President Harry Truman, "The buck stops here!"

1. Share some encouraging parenting skills you learned from your parents and have also put into action with your children.

2. Did you have struggles with the way you were parented in childhood, yet are now able to revisit those memories from a place of peace? Can you write out your process of healing?

3. Take a few moments to reflect on the Soul Food verse (Proverbs 3:5). Do other scriptures come to mind on the topic of leaning on God and trusting Him to work out the details of your life? Which ones have been helpful to read in your role as a daughter or parent?

10

Gratitude Attitude

*It is the sweet simple things in life
which are the real ones after all.*
—Laura Ingalls Wilder

One of my desires is a continued attempt to make the act of being thankful a daily process, with emphasis on the word "attempt." It may start with my morning devotion, but if I missed that it may be at time of getting that amazing parking spot, which suddenly appeared in the mass of what looked liked a no-win situation. Aren't those the best?

One Monday morning in mid March, I had slept later than usual and missed seeing my husband Tom before he left for work. I headed out through the family room, raising window blinds as I went. As I was approaching the kitchen island, I spotted it! Smack dab in the middle of the island was the Panini Maker. It sat there, just as Tom had left it the night before, dirty and wide open to cool off. Okay, I gave him kudos for remembering to do the "cooling off" thing. But from these domestic engineering eyes all I saw was its gaping sneer, saying, "Yes, I am still here and still dirty." I grumbled as I did the easy cleanup. Yes, you read it right, easy cleanup. Within five minutes of this occurrence, my husband called my cell phone and reminded me it was Monday morning and he missed me. Catching on? Well, I hadn't quite yet.

Sitting down with my coffee and opening my devotional, I read, "Let thankfulness temper all your thoughts." Further on, the words "grumble and gratitude" came into the text. As I slid further into my chair . . . I was finally getting it.

Now back to the raising of the blinds . . .

Had I been in my gratitude attitude, I might have noticed our amazing Colorado sun shining down on the snow-covered fairway trees or the bright sky-blue backdrop while raising those blinds. Maybe even feeling a bit more thankful that Tom had quietly allowed me extra sleep time. What a guy, right? Furthermore, his phone call, which he is faithful to do almost every Monday morning by nine a.m., could have been better received and therefore more of an encouragement right back at him.

With thoughtful deliberation I ask you, can we ever be thankful enough? How much more encouragement can we bring to others than by waking up each morning and, before our feet touch that floor, make the decision to have an attitude of gratitude.

PS. After my devotion I did send a text to my husband and thanked him for his faithful call. I am easily convicted.

Soul Food

"Be joyful always; pray continually; give thanks in all circumstances, for this is God's will for you in Christ Jesus."

(I THESSALONIANS 5:16-18 ESV)

Personal Reflection Or Group Discussion

1. We are all challenged. Sometimes things just set us off. What pushes your button to cause a negative attitude and why? What have you found that helps you turn it around?

2. Do you sometimes feel it is easier to be thankful toward the Lord than others in our lives? Why or why not?

3. I Thessalonians 5:16–18 reminds us that our joy, prayers, and thankfulness should not change with our circumstances or feelings: "Rejoice always, pray continually, give thanks in all circumstances; for this is God's will for you in Christ Jesus." Not easy with our human inclinations! Discuss your perspective on these verses. Note: Paul was not teaching that we should thank God for everything that happens to us, but in *everything*.

Journal, Doodle, Reflect

11

Nice to Meet You

This is something I know; no matter how far you have run,
no matter how long you have been lost,
it is never too late to be found.
—Rene Denfeld, The Child Finder

Recently, I read a book called *The Child Finder* by Rene Denfeld. As well as being an international bestselling author and journalist, Ms. Denfeld is also a licensed investigator specializing in death penalty work. The main character in her book is Naomi, a woman in her late twenties. She is a private investigator with an amazing gift for locating lost and missing children. She has earned a reputation among police and a select group of parents as "the child finder." I found myself fascinated with this story, especially Naomi's ongoing inner struggle. This conflict stemmed from her past, as she, too, once was a lost girl. Another aspect I found interesting was that while in captivity, some of these lost children named themselves. Since many were abducted at such a young age, and their names were either not known or not used by their captors, the identity they once had was soon forgotten.

One case she shares in her book took place in the wintery forests of the Pacific Northwest. Naomi sat on the living room couch in the home of the grieving mother with a missing child. The mother asked her, "How do you know how to find them?" She answered with a luminous smile, "Because I know freedom."

There are so many books and resources on names! Do you remember brainstorming and discussing with your spouse what to name your first child? You thought you had picked the perfect and most unique name until . . . your best friend, or the parents of a child in the church nursery or preschool also had the same wonderful idea? I have to say I found it pretty humorous. By the time number two and three came along, there wasn't as much discussion—just deciding on what seemed right for our family. When I turned sixty, a friend gave me a detailed, handwritten description of the meaning of my name. After reading the strengths and character qualities listed, I thought it would be interesting to give myself an evaluation of how I was doing in each of those areas. Yep, Type A again. Doing that was a big mistake and not at all what my sweet friend had intended. I shut that idea down quickly and made the decision to simply cherish those prophetic words.

Have you given yourself a name that you say in the quiet of your mind, or even audibly "at" yourself when no one is around to hear? Does that name bring a negative connotation? It may be a name that is triggered from something you buried away in your past. We can do a fair amount of damage with the anger and disappointment we put toward ourselves in "loose" thoughts. Whatever name you may be addressing yourself by, be assured, this is what your name *is not*:

Slave: The chains were broken when you chose Christ. *(Galatians 5:1)*

Lost: He has never left your side or lost sight of you. *(Hebrews 13:5–6)*

Forsaken: You are a daughter of the One True King. *(Revelation 1:5–6)*

Unworthy/Unloved: Redeemed and restored by His blood, held by His hands. *(Ephesians 1:7)*

Hopeless: Blessed are the poor in spirit, for theirs is the kingdom of Heaven. *(Matthew 5:3)*

Misplaced: He created you in His Image and you are His. God doesn't make mistakes! *(Genesis 1:27)*

Weak: His power is made perfect in your weakness. *(2 Corinthians 12:9)*

Failure: When keeping your eyes upon Him, failure isn't in the vocabulary. *(Hebrews 12:2–3)*

Our Heavenly Father brings the stars out each night and calls them by name. When we chose to put our faith in Christ, God called us out of the darkness and our names were written in His Book of Life. I wonder, when we come face to face with the Lord and He speaks our name, will it sound much different than in everyday life? Coming from His lips, it could only be glorious, right? In the meantime, I am praying that we push aside any negative name-calling the evil one may whisper and take those loose thoughts captive to Christ. The next time you look in the mirror and see that beautiful reflection, say, "I am a created beauty made in His image—loved, redeemed, and the restored daughter of the One True King." It may come to be a reflection of someone you haven't seen in a long while. Praise God!

Soul Food

"Are your ears awake? Listen. Listen to the Wind Words, the Spirit blowing through the churches. I'll give the sacred manna to every conqueror; I'll also give a clear, smooth stone inscribed with your new name, your secret new name."

(REVELATION 2:17 MSG)

Personal Reflection Or Group Discussion

The subject of names is an interesting topic. From birth it is a word by which a person is known and continues onto the one's reputation into adulthood. Additional names (nicknames) can come to us brought about by a person or persons who make fun of someone in a playful or unkind manner.

1. Have you thought of changing the name you were given at birth? What was the motive behind that change?

2. Have you ever given yourself a name when disappointed or angry at something you did or during an unpleasant phase in your life? Perhaps it is when something negative is triggered from your past? Can you put that thought into perspective with what the author listed as "what your name IS NOT?"

3. Share your thoughts on the quote by Rene Denfeld at the beginning of this chapter: "This is something I know; no matter how far you have run, no matter how long you have been lost, it is never too late to be found."

Journal, Doodle, Reflect

12

Fears and Fences

You are beautiful. You are strong.
You are a woman-turned-warrior,
trained by the King
for the very battle that is in front of you.
You got this
—Author unknown

Last evening, we were pleasantly surprised by lightning and thunderstorm, which was followed by a gentle rain. Very unusual this time of year considering it is the middle of winter here in Colorado. We awoke to snow, just barely covering the grass in our yard, and the winds blowing. I am sitting at my desk—window open, coffee in hand. Those who know me well can vouch that winter is my least favorite of the seasons. Yet, I find peace and solace as I listen and watch the antics of the whirlwind out my office window. My patio swing, swaying, beckons to me. I can see the Linden tree in our back yard; its bare branches are in constant movement. The aged cottonwoods upon the fairway, trunks so large and sturdy, their branches waving as the wind whips through them. I spy a few remaining brown leaves left on my favorite tree; I wonder if they will last the storm? When the elements are storming on the outside, I feel peace, contentment, and sometimes even joy. It is simply because I feel safe. I have strong windows and walls protecting me. I have the choice to place myself on the protected side of those barriers. I can see and enjoy all that is unfolding outside, knowing no harm will come to me. Psalm 149 states, "Praise the LORD from the earth . . . lightening and hail, snow and clouds, stormy winds that do his bidding" (vv.7–8).

I have not always felt safe in my life. I am not speaking of the physical aspect, but the mental and emotional part in which fear can subtly take control. Fear can become the lie of "protection" we hide behind, keeping our hearts stagnant, barricading us from living the life God desires for us.

In conversations I've had with women who were willing to discuss the struggles in their lives, the subject of fear is one that stands out as most common above all. What I heard is that it wasn't something that just happened in a short span of time; for some it began during childhood and took a snowball effect as the years went on. For others, it came about during years of marriage, raising children, and trying to live life as they thought others perceived them. Fear had reached a point of consuming their thoughts and affecting their everyday actions and relationships. We live in a fallen world, where satan can run havoc with our lives if allowed. I believe fear is the enemy's stronghold in many of our lives. Too often, his attacks occur at our weakest moments and in varied and unsuspecting ways. I can also personally vouch that he will take his time to make his mark. The Apostle Peter says, "Stay alert! Watch out for your great enemy, the devil. He prowls around like a roaring lion, looking for someone to devour" (I Peter 5:8 NLT).

My father joined the navy before graduating from high school. While still in the Navy, he and my mother were married, and I came along a few years later. We lived the first few years of my life in a small house that adjoined property with my father's parent's home in a tiny town in Washington State. I can still remember walking the cow coral with my grandma Shirley and her black-and-white boxer named Rocky. I still love the smell of farm manure!

My favorite memory is sitting upon my grandma's kitchen floor with a big, yellow ceramic bowl and a large wooden spoon, savoring the chocolate frosting used for the homemade chocolate cake she had just baked. Her kitchen was a safe place. The love of chocolate still remains with me! I cherish those long ago special memories.

Later, we moved to Horse Heaven Hills, a few miles outside of Kennewick, Washington. There were miles and miles of golden wheat fields and dirt roads. My dad had a strong personality. He was also a handsome man and a hard worker. He drove harvest combines on the wheat ranches where we lived, owned by two of his uncles. He was a welder, broke horses, and was even a farrier for his own personal horses. Some might say he was the definition of a man's man. He came from the old school of thought that raising children was a woman's job, and since his firstborn was a daughter and not a son, I suppose that even cemented his belief further. From what has been described to me over the years, I would say that while my parents were raised in very different environments, they held a common bond of family pain and dysfunction growing up. Sadly, their marriage was destined for destruction from the beginning. I still picture myself as a little girl hiding behind the big, brown furnace in our living room hearing hurtful words and angry accusations resonating through our home. That may have been my first feeling that something wasn't quite right.

My parents divorced when I was eight years old. After that, my mother, younger sister, and I moved to another town twenty minutes away. Visits with our dad were scattered, usually over holidays or birthday events. Even though I knew in my heart the three of us were in a healthier environment, I still missed him. What would I do without a daddy? There was fear when I was with him and fear when I was without him. The circumstance made for a very insecure little girl. The lie that fear was part of me had been set in place. The internal barriers around my heart and soul began to construct. That lie wove its way into many areas of my life for many years. Jesus says that when the devil speaks, "he makes it up out of his lying nature and fills the world with lies" (John 8:44 MSG). Author Jasona Brown phrases it so perfectly in her book *Stone by Stone*: "The enemy of my soul had begun his assault. Trauma churns up our need to make meaning out of life: Why did this happen? What does this mean about me? About God?"

When I was older, I was more intentional about getting to know my dad. Even as I write this, I am sad to say the relationship has never been what I would have desired. There are times in our lives when we have to let go and acknowledge

God is in control. Many times I have prayed to have an open heart and mind to a particular situation and asked God to help me see it through His eyes. I have faith that the Lord in His sovereign way has protected me from additional hurt.

The next significant fear, which hit me like "walking into a wall," occurred within the first two months of marriage. My husband Tom and I were enjoying a leisurely Saturday morning when my tears began to flow. He looked over at me with panic in his eyes (maybe wondering if I was regretting it all!). I tearfully said, "I'm afraid I don't believe our marriage can work. There is so much generational pain and divorce in my family background." I had begun to doubt God's plan. I had prayed fervently in the past, asking the Lord to bring the man He desired me to marry into my life. The man of God's choosing was right here, yet I just couldn't release this fear and doubt. Tom took me in his arms and tenderly reassured me we were "breaking the chain." I trusted and believed him. Without that fear, I could allow myself to be the wife God wanted me to be. Of course, breaking the chain is an ongoing process. I will never attain relational perfection, but it is a welcomed challenge to keep trying!

The third ongoing fear I experience is leaving this world behind. Many of you may read this and say, "Is she serious? I can't wait to leave this crazy world and head for heaven!" I know Scripture calls us to not love the world or anything in the world more than God (1 John 2:15). I often imagine the time when I will stand before the throne of my amazing Creator and feel His loving embrace. And yet, I do hold dear the special relationships God has allowed me to experience—

the gifts of my husband, children, and grandchildren. I also love experiencing God's creation in the four seasons wherever I am residing at the time. I am in awe and so eternally grateful for my sight, hearing, and sense of touch. I have a simplistic yet beautiful worldview, and I am grateful God chose to instill this in my character. Sarah Young captures my feelings about the duality of earthly life and heavenly life in *Jesus Calling* "I made you in My image, and I hid heaven in your heart. Your yearning for Me is a form of homesickness: longing for your true home in Heaven." Note: I am in conversation with God about this; it seems to be getting easier with age, but it's not yet resolved. ☺

I have great respect for my longtime and dear friend Gail, who (along with other titles) is a life coach. For those of you who may not be familiar with this profession, I will try to define it in a few brief sentences. A life coach guides and supports people who are confused about which direction to steer their life. They help others set achievable goals and assist in behavior modification to bring about positive changes in their lives. A life coach's ability to move others forward comes about by asking intentional questions, establishing accountability, and offering insight instead of advice. Gail has a saying she came across several years back to give her clients perspective. In its simplicity, it is quite profound: "If nothing changes, nothing changes." A few years ago I asked Gail what she has observed in her practice as a common fear among women. She didn't have to hesitate long before answering, "One of the greatest fears of women, when having to make a life-changing decision, is thinking, *I can't handle it!*" She further explained to me that belief holds us back from pursuing anything we want or something we have never done. That is also why confidence comes in the "doing" and only when there is action.

How many different fears do you live with or hide behind? Do you allow those fears to keep you from the action of moving forward? Ask the Lord to open your heart to hear what the Holy Spirit desires to speak to your soul. God sees the beautiful person inside of you, created in His image with no fear and intimidation, full of joy and anticipation. Break the barrier and be you!

Soul Food

"The LORD is my light and my salvation—whom shall I fear? The LORD is the stronghold of my life—of whom shall I be afraid?"

(PSALM 27:1)

Personal Reflection Or Group Discussion

1. The author shared three of her fears, which spread over a period of time in her life. What is one fear that presently or in the past has haunted you and why?

2. Describe the internal barriers you constructed to help ease the pain of your fear. Were they helpful? Why or why not?

3. What do you think of the author's comment that fear can
    become the enemy's stronghold in our lives? Read and
    discuss 1 Peter 5:8.

Journal, Doodle, Reflect

13

Worry Web

*Even in the midst of the day's difficulties
and challenges, may I continue to be in anticipation
of His eternal perspective of it all.*
—Teresa Alley

I believe many fears can begin with the simple act of worry. We live in a fallen world where, if allowed, satan can have a field day with our minds. Our everyday lives are filled with all sorts of issues, sometimes bringing about anxiety and worry. That which starts out as a small, negative thought can spin out of control and quickly emerge into what I call a worry web. The threads of this worry web can lead to lack of hope and trust, anxiousness, and lack of motivation to move forward with life—unenterprising!

Oswald Chambers, in *My Utmost For His Highest*, states, "Fretting means getting ourselves 'out of joint' mentally or spiritually." He later goes on to explain how worrying comes from our determination of wanting things our way and always results in sin. That led me to take time and test this for myself. When I worry, what could be some of the sinful results? Do I think God can't handle the situation? Foolishly lacking faith.

Worrying allows my mind to wander, taking on a snowball effect. This can bring my anxiety to unhealthy levels for both mind and body.

Worrying takes my mind and efforts away from other priorities.

Worrying spurns me on to handle the issue myself without waiting upon the Lord.

My worrying, when shared inappropriately, could cause others to stumble.

Often when I journal, I draw pictures or symbols of how God speaks to me about my thoughts or struggles. When my children were young and I would pray for them, I visualized putting them upon God's altar. They are His first, so who knows better for them then their Creator? I still do that today, even though they are all adults. It truly gives me a sense of peace.

Not long ago I realized the worry issue had subtly crept back into my life. I knew I couldn't set it aside, as some of the worries were not only affecting my personal and family life, but also hindering me in the writing of this book. Unfortunately, I have witnessed people who were slaves to fear. In time, it encompassed a large part of who they were. One of the biggest factors I noticed in their lives was the lack of joy. That spoke right to my heart.

As I put my web design together, I asked the Holy Spirit to reveal some of the worries I may not have identified. Let me say it was not one of my more enjoyable journal writings, nor did I complete the task in just one morning. Yet once it was finished, I did feel the weight lifted, and I knew the Holy Spirit was directing me toward a more positive and productive place.

Soul Food

"Who of you by worrying can add a single hour to his life?"

(MATTHEW 6:27)

Personal Reflection Or Group Discussion

1. It is so easy to struggle with worry, anxiousness, and negative thoughts in some form or another. Can you give an example of how you have seen one or all of these actions take on the form of sin in your life? Refer to the author's list of "sinful results."

2. "Who of you by worrying can add a single hour to his life?" (Matthew 6:27). Does this scripture speak to you personally? If so, how?

3. CREATIVE THOUGHT! Do you journal, doodle, or reflect? Have you considered doing so in your quiet times with the Lord?

Journal, Doodle, Reflect

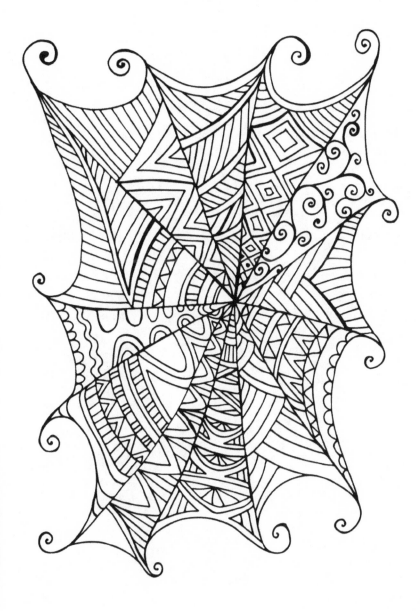

14

S.O.S.

As you wait upon the Lord, you learn to see things from His perspective, move at His pace, and function under His directives.

—Roy Lessi

*S*oul. It is one of my favorite words. For me, it represents the place where only God can touch. It is where my intimate communication with Him occurs. It is the place where the Holy Spirit dwells faithfully and continually, guiding me toward the Lord. It is the inevitable part of me that will join Him in Eternity.

How loud is your quiet? One of my favorite places to engage in what I call Stillness of Soul (S.O.S.) is on the swing that hangs on my back patio. There have been two swings purchased over the years from my family to me as a Mother's Day gift. The first had a wooden frame, which, even after a second paint job, didn't last long with the hot Colorado summer sun. The next and present swing is made of coated metal, equipped with a comfy cushion and two small pillows. From spring until late fall (and even on some winter days), coffee cup in hand, it's Jesus and me. It isn't entirely silent, as many mornings the birds are singing their way through the trees, or I may hear the distant sound of fairway mowers on the golf course. But those familiar sounds warm my heart and bring me a feeling of contentment instead of distraction. I have a friend who has a special chair in her family room. She is able to swivel the chair, turning her back on the rest of the room, and look out a large picture window at a lovely pond. Another friend has turned a small room in her home to a place to meet with God, calling it her Sacred Place. Establishing a meeting place with God, inside your home or outside in nature, is key in fulfilling the commitment to stay connected to Him. This scripture confirms our need for connection: "The Lord your God is with you, the Mighty Warrior who saves. He will take great delight in you; in his love he will no longer rebuke you, but will rejoice over you with singing" (Zephaniah 3:17).

From the Old Testament Israelites to the first century Christians, commandments of waiting on God tell us we can experience hope, salvation, and the eventual joy of heaven. And yet, I still find it is not an easy thing to accomplish. Our spirits can be squelched in one brief, instantaneous thought. There are so many loud distractions—time factors, the ever-present to-do lists and the inner voices that guilt us because of those to-dos! When was the last time you experienced the type of silence that allows you to feel God's presence in such a way that brings rejuvenation to your soul, where all of your being comes before Him and . . . waits? God deserves nothing less.

Psalm 130:5 says, "I wait for the Lord, my soul waits, and in his word I put my hope." How is it that I have the audacity, without first coming before His presence, to think I can make better choices for myself than God can? In truth, I cannot. When I trust my own understanding above His knowledge, things are bound to go off track, and even worse, I most likely won't handle it with the grace and acceptance that honors Him. I don't want to be wishing my day away for something else or fighting the hours until my head hits the pillow with thoughts of, *Today was a waste, but tomorrow is another day.* I desire to look at each day and its circumstances with the feeling of anticipation. My first thought should be, *This is the day the Lord has made, and He is on the move!*

I continually ask the Lord, " Even in the midst of the day's difficulties and challenges, help me to be in anticipation of the eternal perspective of it all." Is this an easy act of trust? Not always. Is it a bit risky? By the world's standards—absolutely! But it's definitely hopeful beyond expectation! Engage your S.O.S. and wait in anticipation for His next move.

Soul Food

"Quiet, everyone! Shh! Silence before GOD. Something's afoot in his holy house. He's on the move!"

(ZECHARIAH 2:13 MSG)

Personal Reflection Or Group Discussion

I read through an old journal and came across this reflective statement I wrote: "A time for everything, and everything in His time." As you finish this chapter, be open to what these words might illuminate in your life. What do they speak to you about patience, trust, endurance, and faith?

1. In all honesty, waiting on the Lord can be tough to do. We are people who are use to getting what we want, when we want it. How is your patience level with this action?

2. Stillness of Soul (S.O.S.) is a time when the author quiets herself and welcomes God into her space for reflection, inspiration, and renewal. What do you find is your greatest distraction when desiring to engage in this exercise?

3. CHALLENGE: Would your outlook on difficult, unpleasant, or even the mundane events of the everyday life look different if you could be in the habit of asking God, "What is the eternal perspective of this situation?" Are you willing to try?

Journal, Doodle, Reflect

15

Stuck at 60 – Can We Talk?

*I may infuse within you a dream that seems far
beyond your reach. You know that in yourself you cannot
achieve such a goal. Thus begins your journey
of profound reliance on Me.*
—Jesus Calling, Sarah Young

The year I turned sixty was not a favorite of my aging years. That year included personal losses of family members, serious reoccurring health issues for friends, marriages of people I loved scattering in all directions, and the political world—domestic and global—was topsy-turvy. I realize that none of these issues are out of the ordinary for the majority of the population, and I do not make light of that. But the basis of this book is encouragement, and this chapter is about sharing my vulnerabilities. So, as the loved and belated comedian Joan Rivers use to say, "Can we talk?"

Before there was even a discussion of a party for my sixtieth birthday, I had asked to keep it simple. I knew my family would go for an all-out birthday bash if I was agreeable, but I truly wanted intimate time with immediate family only. It's not often you can get three adult kids plus a spouse and their parents together for an entire evening! Over appetizers and wine, my kids proceeded to celebrate, honor, and encourage me with a list of sixty different characteristics and personal adjectives they felt described me, as well as our individual relationship with one another. I was overwhelmed and humbled. During the course of dinner my son Mark asked, "So Mom, how is the book coming along?" I responded, "I have a strong feeling I will have it finished by Christmas," Little did I know, the saga of my "stuck and stagnant" period was just beginning. Sixty— *whoa!*—it was settling in.

Weeks leading up to my birthday, I had been experiencing many unsettling feelings. I considered the fact that I tend to struggle with the holiday season in general. My birthday being early December, and with holidays already upon us, I could easily put the blame there for my paralyzed state of mind. Of course, hormones are always a good excuse, except that I had already been there and done that in my early fifties. Nor was it the act of saying my age aloud if someone asked. As the days and weeks moved forward, I realized turning sixty was a reality I wasn't handling well.

After much discussion with myself, I concluded it was the simple fact that statistically, according to CBS News in 2016, my life expectancy was three-fourths of the way done! I know the Lord decides my number of days, and He will call me home in His time. I was good with all that. But the wife, mother of adult children, and nana of two precious grandsons was questioning his timing. Have I done all that God has wanted me to do with all the gifts He has given me? Have I thoroughly shared with my children and others the details of what Christ's unconditional love has done for me over my lifetime? Does my husband of thirty-eight years truly know the depth of my love for him? Does my forgiveness of those in my life need to be extended beyond something greater than I have allowed in my heart? Bottom line, what kind of legacy was I leaving, when I leave? And the end of that thought process was: Where do I go from this "stuck" state of being?

You may wonder where I was with the Lord in all this contemplation. Honestly, I was avoiding Him. Sound familiar? Listening to the quiet, negative whispers of the evil one, I felt I was moving backward, or at least at a standstill. I had lost confidence in what God had placed upon my heart, one of which was the writing of this book. There begins the process to open the door, allowing satan to begin his subtle attack. And therein is where things can begin to crumble.

The Bible gives us a great example of this in Genesis 19. Two angels arrived in the city of Sodom and visited Lot. In the process of them staying with Lot and his family, the angels were actually protecting them so they could safely head out of the city into the mountains. Why did they need protection? Because the Lord was planning to destroy the two cities of Sodom and Gomorrah with a sulfur rain. Yikes! Lot was a deal maker and asked that the nearby city, Zoar, be spared so his family could make the trek there. Apparently Lot wasn't up for hiking the mountain that night, so the angels mercifully guided them out of the city at dawn. They then urged them forward with specific instructions: "Don't look back, and don't stop anywhere" (v. 17). But Lot's wife, clinging to the memories of the past, had to look back. She immediately became a pillar of salt and crumbled. This is a strong message for a number of reasons, but the main idea is that looking back may not always be the best avenue!

The bottom line is, I needed to remind myself to move forward and reclaim those dreams and desires. First is regrouping. What are my priorities and my personal desires? Second, I need to prayerfully seek God's priorities for my life. That may seem a bit backward, but it works well for me as I converse with God, journal, listen, and wait for Him to reveal His plan. Sometimes communing with God can feel routine and monotonous, but other times He takes me in an exciting new direction!

I believe there is always time to stop, re-evaluate, and change directions. My golfing gals and I have said too many times after hitting a bad shot, "I knew that setup didn't feel right. If I just would have stepped back . . ." In golf, decisions are made in a matter of seconds to keep up with the speed of play. But in the game of life, there is no timeline designated with that simple concept. A favorite poet of mine, Robert Louis Stevenson, wrote it so well: "The best things in life are nearest; breath in your nostrils, light in your eyes, flowers at your feet, duties in your hand, and the path of God just before you."

I am thankful for the qualities, some more simplistic than others, which the Lord has given me. It defines who I am and who I continue to become beyond my age.

Soul Food

"Hope deferred makes the heart sick, but a longing fulfilled is a tree of life."

(PROVERBS 13:12)

Personal Reflection Or Group Discussion

1. So far, what has been your favorite age and why?

2. Have you spent time periodically looking back on your life? Were you able to glean the Lord's perspective of the "how and whys" of different occurrences?

3. If comfortable, share some dreams you desire for yourself. Are you still pursuing those dreams?

Journal, Doodle, Reflect

16

Leave Behind, Future Forward

Looking back you realize that a very special person passed briefly through your life—and it was you. It's not too late to find that person again.
—Robert Brault, author

There are times when examining our past and learning from mistakes can be such a healthy and healing series of steps. I did discover, through trial and many errors, examination for me occurs best when my mind and soul are in a positive place with the Lord. Of course, if that "happy place" just doesn't seem to be happening, a trustworthy counselor may be the next step.

As I mentioned earlier, looking back can also have negative effects. Besides the possibility of being changed into a pillar of salt, let's pepper that with the guilt, anger, sadness, self-doubt, and regret we can put upon ourselves. It may even be such a distraction that we entirely miss the course or direction God has placed before us. Part of that experience, which was most difficult for me, is that I lost myself. Clouded with uncertainty, I allowed unpleasant and painful thoughts of the past to settle in my mind. I had allowed a spark to flame, and it was like a wildfire in a dense and dry forest. At times, I truly felt as if I was someone else. Mentally "in hiding" from God, I began to feel a form of hopelessness.

Is there something that haunts you and keeps you shackled by past sins? Have you given up on the idea of hope? Do you think you missed the path He set before you long ago? Remember that Christ has already been there for us. He left heaven and entered the darkness of this world—the price is paid! Though we cannot change the past, we have the choice to begin each day as something new: future forward.

For over thirty years, my husband and I have supported a ministry in Denver called Providence Network. Providence Network helps men, women, and families heal from addictions, domestic violence, and homelessness while continuing to encourage and provide the skills to become self-sufficient and productive members of the community. While attending a fundraiser luncheon in October of 2013, one of the speakers, who was a resident of one of the homes owned by Providence, gave his testimony. This young man had struggled with addiction for a number of years. He was now seven years sober and had achieved his goal of becoming an emergency room nurse. He had struggled with addiction for a number of years. He shared his story of how the staff of Providence had loved and accepted him while giving him the support to become the man God had created him to be. But here was the amazing part to his story—during those years of struggle, he had been in and out of Providence Network many times and they never gave up on him! He had just completed a bike race beginning on the Golden Gate Bridge in San Francisco and ending on the Brooklyn Bridge in New York to raise money and awareness for those who are fighting alcohol and drug addiction. At the end of his presentation, his simple yet profound words brought tears to my eyes: "I now enjoy showing up for my life." He once again had Hope! Praise God.

As I mentioned earlier (S.O.S.), my mantra of hope continues: "Even in the midst of the day's difficulties and challenges, may I continue to be in anticipation of the eternal perspective of it all." The wondrous and amazing truth is that Jesus sees us as we are and, more important, all that we can be. He knows us—who and where we've been. David Crowder's song, "Come As You Are," speaks of kneeling before God with your sadness, brokenness, burdens, and shame and lifting your face to heaven, receiving mercy just as you are. Will you make the choice and be willing to let God start something brand new? No big changes required!

Soul Food

"Forget about what's happened; don't keep going over old history. Be alert. Be present. I'm about to do something brand-new."

(ISAIAH 43:18-19 MSG)

Personal Reflection Or Group Discussion

1. Have you ever experienced a time in your life when you felt as though you lost yourself? Write out what word pictures come to mind of what that looked like.

2. During this period, did you feel there was something or someone specific that kept you from moving forward?

3. CHALLENGE: Thoughtfully read Isaiah 43:18-19 (soul food). Can you commit these words to the Lord and use them in your everyday life?

Journal, Doodle, Reflect

17

God Knows Us

I can't hide from Your presence, though many times I've tried.
You know what I dream, when I wake, and when I rise.

My thoughts and actions sadly, sometimes bring me shame it's true.
Yet, through Your grace and forgiving love I start each day anew.

You see my thoughts before I speak, my actions so well known.
Each day Your right hand holds me fast, I'm never all alone.

How can I be surprised at Your knowledge of my days?
How vast the sum of all Your thoughts, how powerful Your ways.

In the secret depths of the earth, my inmost being became a plan,
Lovingly placed in my mother's womb by the miracle of
Your hands.
Cell by cell encased by my frame, and I became a whole.
And last, the most important, was the grafting of my soul.

Written down before they came to be, my days
You then ordained.
Uniquely made, compared to none, redeemed from guilt
and shame.

Seeking Your wisdom and truth, always a challenging
aspiration.
I am so grateful for Your Word and Your Spirit's discerning
direction.

I call upon you Lord to test and search my every thought.
Examine all that stands before You and calm my anxious heart.

My ever faithful Father, Elohim, Yahweh,
Most High,
And in Your time, You'll call me home, Your arms held
open wide!
—Teresa Alley

Soul Food

"So God created mankind in his own image, in the image of God he created them; male and female he created them."

(GENESIS 1:27)

Personal Reflection Or Group Discussion

1. The author alluded to "hiding from God" both in chapter 16 and in the poem in chapter 17. Give your explanation of what hiding from God looks like to you.

2. Read stanza nine: "I call upon you Lord to test and search my every thought. Examine all that stands before You and calm my anxious heart." What emotions do you feel (uneasy, secure, challenged, safe)?

3. Stanza six speaks of God and His miraculous process of creating us. Take a few moments to appreciate when you were being formed in your mother's womb. Write down as many of the unique and positive characteristics God lovingly gave to you.

18

What If?

Love has been called the most effective motivational force
in all the world. Where love is at work in us
it is remarkable how giving and forgiving,
understanding and tolerant we can be.
—Charles Swindoll

—You've got to be kidding. Do you have any idea how angry she has made me? Not to mention the fact she spoke falsely about me behind my back to others.

—He is our leader, manager of the office, and I now question his motives as well as his integrity almost daily. I feel I was given a false impression when he hired me.

—She calls herself my good friend. I've been there for her when she needs me. She, on the other hand, is unreliable. She never asks or seems to care about the struggles in my life.

—My family was violently taken from me in a matter of moments. How could God possibly expect me to forgive?

—We gave our vows with love, for better or worse. He has lied, cheated, broken the vows, and broken me.

—It wasn't fair that I had to grow up so fast. I still resent the fact of childhood innocence passing me by.

This list of examples and more could fill pages. Most of us had experiences in our lives where we found ourselves in anger, grief, hurt, despair, and even disbelief over someone whom we felt wronged us in some form. Our first instinct, usually done out of anger, is to make that person/persons aware of their hurtful actions toward us. Give it right back—done deal! But God strongly cautions us about that in Scripture. "Don't insist on getting even; that's not for you to do. I'll do the judging," says God. "I'll take care of it" (Romans 12:19 MSG).

In writing this chapter, I had discussions with a number of women friends about how they handle "tough forgiveness." Here are a few statements that were common among them: "I try and forget what happened, if I can, and let time pass. Sometimes that is the easiest way for me to forgive." "I found it easier to forgive my husband, who had been unfaithful, than a friend who had purposely been antagonistic and hurtful toward me. My husband was extremely remorseful, whereas my friend was not."

My own personal experience in the past has been to hold a grudge with an underlying feeling of resentment. I tried to minimize it, never giving the impression that there was any kind of an issue. Over time, I allowed a silent, slow festering of bitterness to grow in my heart. When you carry that around for a good length of time, it begins to permeate other areas of your life. Hebrews 12:15 gives us good advice, "Keep a sharp eye out for weeds of bitter discontent. A thistle or two gone to seed can ruin a whole garden in no time" (MSG).

Several years ago, I heard a speaker make the statement that true forgiveness is rare. Quietly and too quickly, I challenged that idea until I took the time to give it some thought. When I forgive, is it always a genuine act coming from my heart? The honest answer was no! I realized that for me learning to forgive was a definite process. First, I had to acknowledge the Holy Spirit's prompting of where my attitude was. Second, I had to change my attitude. This was a tough one. I asked Christ to help me see those who had caused me pain through His eyes. In one instance I sought a counselor who was very helpful in giving me a different perspective regarding a sensitive (and most likely unchangeable) situation with a family member in my life. Third, I had to revisit and review the pain of the present/past and release it. I can truly say, while not easy in the beginning, each occasion brought a greater sense of freedom— an oppression lifted and gone.

Romans 12:18 says, "If it is possible, as far as it depends on you, live at peace with everyone." This doesn't mean we are excusing or forgetting, just forgiving and loving people in spite of their sins, as Christ continues to do for us.

Soul Food

"Be kind and compassionate to one another, forgiving each other, just as in Christ God forgave you."

(EPHESIANS 4:32)

Questions for Reflections or Group Discussions

In Matthew 6:9–13, Christ gives us a pattern to use for prayer. "This, then, is how you should pray: "'Our Father in heaven, hallowed be your name, your kingdom come, your will be done, on earth as it is in heaven. Give us today our daily bread. And forgive us our debts, as we also have forgiven our debtors. And lead us not into temptation, but deliver us from the evil one.' "

1. The Lord's Prayer (specifically verse 12) asks us to come before Him and ask for forgiveness with the same condition of our heart in which we forgive others. Do you personally struggle with asking God for forgiveness and accepting His grace? If so, has it made it even harder to forgive others?

2. The author shared the steps she took dealing with forgiveness. Do you have a forgiveness narrative you could share that may help others?

3. What does the quote at the beginning of this chapter say to you relating to forgiveness?

Journal, Doodle, Reflect

19

Unimaginable Forgiveness

In the darkness of Gethsemane a betrayal kiss was sadly given.
One of many salvific events God planed for mankind's
way to heaven.

Priests and elders came for Your arrest, carrying with them
swords and chains.
Your only challenge were the words, "This is your hour—when
Satan reigns."

A third denial and the rooster crows, Your fate is falling
into place.
You turn to see sorrowful weeping as You look upon
Peter's guilty face.

Scorning you with a crown of thorns, beatings and
insults mockingly.
They taunted, "Release yourself from our chains with who you
claim to be."

Daybreak, the council asked, "Are you the Christ,
King of the Jews, God's only Son?"
You spoke the truth for all to hear, "I AM the Holy One."

"Blasphemy and crucify," came zealous demand from
those around.
Shouts prevailed—Pilate fearfully surrendered, submitting to
the crowd.

Oh Lord, it grieves me so to think of Your suffering and
other's disloyal denials.
Would I have shown the courage to be a faithful witness
at Your trials?

Down streets of Jerusalem, bruised and bloodied,
You took Your final steps.
To the hill of Golgotha, unjustly crucified between
two men condemned.

As You hung and bled upon that cross, Roman soldiers
divided up Your clothes,
And then my sweet Messiah, You asked God's forgiveness
for their souls.

I have sadness and anger at all who participated
in this treacherous plan!

Yet, I am not one innocent, knowing my future sins
were upon the Son of Man.

You sent Your Holy Spirit of Truth to counsel our
hearts and minds,
Help me Spirit to grant this same forgiveness,
the Father graciously designed.
                              —Teresa Alley

Soul Food

"Then he said, 'Jesus, remember me when you come
into your kingdom.' Jesus answered him, 'I tell you
the truth, today you will be with me in paradise.' "
                    (LUKE 23:42-43)

Personal Reflection Or Group Discussion

You are a time traveler and a Christian. You are placed
in the described situations from the poem and witness
Jesus being betrayed, denied, scorned, and mocked.
You hear people asking for His death.

1. Place yourself in one of those situations and describe
    how you may have reacted to what you were witnessing.
    (Don't go beyond stanza six.)

2. You are now following behind Jesus as He makes His way to the hill of Golgotha. You can hear His labored breathing and see His bloodied back from being flogged. Listen to Him and share what you *don't* hear.

3. Jesus is crucified. He focuses on *your* face in the crowd. He speaks to you directly. What does He say? Hint: Read Matthew 6:14-15, Romans 12:17, and Colossians 3:13.

20

Southwestern Chicken Chowder

I value the friend who for me finds time on his calendar,
but I cherish the friend who for me does not
consult his calendar.
—Robert Brault, author

On the first Friday of December, Marie, a dear friend of mine hosts her annual "Soups On" party in Centennial, Colorado. She began this tradition over thirty years ago. I am one among many women invitees who rarely miss this event. The choice of three different soups, breads, and a variety of homemade desserts are delightfully scrumptious. My favorite so far is the Southwestern Chicken Chowder. But here is the best part: I have witnessed seeing the joy in her eyes that comes from watching what women do best—taking time to enjoy the act of fellowship. I would guess she would agree with me when I say she cherishes this event.

In March of 2015, *The Today Show* shared research that had been gathered on the emotional health of men and women. For men, the number one form of security was being married. Part of the data reported was that while men valued their male friendships, most of those relationships were based on doing some sort of physical activity—sports, fishing, hunting, golf. Overall, women found their greatest security and encouragement spending time in deep-seated friendships with girlfriends.

Yet, finding those types of friendships as adults does not come as easy as some may think. Marla Paul's *The Friendship Crisis* speaks to this issue. In her search, she found that having a "friendship shortage" is quite common, especially in a major lifestyle change. She gives examples of moving to a new city, perhaps you have a family and others you meet do not, or you are working from home. In response to her writing, many women commented they were relieved to find they weren't the only ones. "It was kind of like I opened the door on this shameful secret—that it is really hard to make friends as you get older," she says.

Likewise, I remember being in my thirties and having older women friends serve as mentors. These were women who were solid in their faith and were willing to share wisdom from their mistakes. They helped balance me out when I was questioning so many things about being a wife and mother.

I have observed that as women age we seem to intentionally have less new friendships. I can attest to this personally. Once I became an empty nester, I had less time with friends then before. I was no longer on a set schedule with kids' activities and commitments. I was able to fill in the spaces with activities I had not previously allowed myself time for. I was able to be a bit more spontaneous. My friendships were still very important, but a more concentrated effort was necessary, thus adding more friendships was a bit more difficult.

As reported in *Time*, June 2017, two different studies were done by author William Chopik on how friendships become increasingly important to health and happiness as people age. "In the first, involving 270,000 people in nearly 100 countries, Chopik found that both family and friend relationships were associated with better health and happiness overall. For the other study, Chopik analyzed a separate survey of nearly 7,500 older people in the US. Here, he found that it wasn't just important to have friends, but that the quality of those friendships also mattered." The author of this article, Amanda MacMillan, stated, "The benefits of having close pals may also be stronger for older people because, by that point, those friendships have stood the test of time." Amen to that!

I am not a huge fan of social media. With that said, texting is a must to keep in contact with my adult children, as well as my favorite pastime, FaceTiming with my grandchildren. Social media is a great tool for immediate connections and large group communication. But, in my opinion, the sad downfall of social media is that it gives a false sense of who and what people are about. We are only allowed to see what people want us to see. What has this done to friendships and relationships?

In the summer of 2016, Mehmet Oz, M.D. and Michael Crupain, M.D., MPH (with the help of political pollster Mike Berland) conducted a survey of women from all around the country to find out the state of women's health in America. They titled the results of that survey "The New Loneliness." Their findings were surprising. With social media we are more "connected" today than in the past. [Yet] "sixty percent of women have feelings of isolation or loneliness and 20% experience this state most or all the time. It's concerning because loneliness is more than just a feeling, it is actually a threat to your health." Their survey concluded that women spent more time reading about what their friends are doing than actually talking to them. A wonderful statement from the article defining friendship is, "true social connectedness involves having deep relationships where we make ourselves vulnerable to our friends who in return make themselves vulnerable to us. Friendship is a two-way street where both need to be honest with each other and give feedback, not just interact superficially and put on a façade."

I am blessed to have shared my life growing up with a sister. We have all heard the saying, "You can't choose your family, but you can choose your friends." I have the best of both worlds. I am five years older than Jami, but when we are together I've often reminded her that it's only mentioned when it is to my advantage. We are extremely close, even though we have lived in separate states since 1978. We have had some "come to Jesus" sessions with one another over the years, which has enriched our relationship and helped build healthy boundaries. I love to organize and she loves to cook, so when we have kitchen time, I may be cleaning out her spice drawer and get a great meal in return.

Recently, I lost a friend to cancer. Carrie had been diagnosed with breast cancer two years before and had been through chemo treatment. She lost her hair and her energy waned, but she never gave up her will to live. She rallied after treatment was over and was able to get back to golf, power walking, and even took a trip to Ireland with her husband and two adult children. Unfortunately the cancer returned; this time in her lungs. She was accepted into a study at the Mayo Clinic in Arizona. She persevered. We were all hopeful. But then after a short period of time, things took a dramatic change and her X-rays showed her lungs were filled with tumors. I was not one of her closest friends, but she graciously allowed me to be of help at times. I was so encouraged by her attitude, never complaining and taking the situation at hand and dealing with it the best she could. Carrie ran the race and she did it with grace and courage. I am so thankful for the time God put her in my life.

Currently, it is a late summer Colorado afternoon, and I am sitting at the kitchen island of Marie's Vail mountain home. The breeze is moving through the Aspen trees outside the window, causing shadows to dance back and forth across the white granite countertop. Through the open door to the patio, I can hear conversation among the women who are here with me. It is our tenth year of this annual trip in Vail. Although we will not be partaking in Marie's delicious chicken chowder during our stay here, we will be sharing lots of latte-laughter and some tears. This has been a relationship in process for over thirty years. We nine women, along with our spouses, are in a Koinonia ("fellowship" in Greek) Bible study group. It began within the first year of marriage for some, and over the following years others joined. As of January 2020, we have twenty-six adult children and thirty-three grandchildren (more on the way). A fruitful group! We have raised children, had ups and downs in marriages, experienced hormonal changes, and even redefined ourselves—maybe more than once. They have talked, prayed, and loved me through many rough situations in my life. What I appreciate even more is their sincere honesty when seeking their advice. I love them for who they are and their desire to continually walk in relationship with Christ. How I cherish each of those women.

I believe God has a special place and plan in His heart for the friendships of women. While creating us in His image, He knew these intimate relationships would be an intricate part of our lives. As young girls, He watched over us as we struggled to find that forever best friend, many times being hurt in the process. We grew and matured, and He waited patiently for us to find our confidence and security in Him. It is important to honor our friendships, yet our dependence has to be on Christ alone.

As in the recipe for Southwestern Chicken Chowder, the different ingredients are important for the delicious outcome. And so it is with the different and genuine friendships God gives us; each one has it's own unique "flavor." You may have friends who like to spice things up and challenge you in ways that pull you out of your comfort zone. There are some, like a wonderful dish of comfort food, whose mere presence can bring us to a full and peaceful place of being. Or maybe, like the once-a-week favorite family entrée, the steady and logical friend we can count on at a moment's notice. This past birthday my sweet friend Terri blessed me with a birthday card, which I think summarizes friendship well:

"The best kind of friend is the comfortable kind. The no fuss, be yourself, take you at face value kind. The listen to you, laugh with you, celebrate the small stuff with you, and help you keep things in perspective kind."

May the Lord shine His Light upon you, as you continue the Circle of Encouragement.

Soul Food

"A man of many companions may come to ruin, but there is a friend who sticks closer than a brother."
(PROVERBS 18:24 ESV)

Personal Reflection Or Group Discussion

1. God sometimes brings people into our lives that we wouldn't necessarily pick for friends, yet this can be a blessing in disguise. Have you experienced this?

2. What are your thoughts about the results of the survey done by Dr. Oz and Dr. Crupain titled "The New Loneliness"?

3. What is one of the best things a friend has done when you were in need?

Journal, Doodle, Reflect

21

Foundational Friendships

Running through the wheat fields, creators of each day,
the barn and abandoned sheds, our perfect place of play.
My formative first friend, so young and sweet and kind,
many of the memories are gone with age and time.

A beautiful, blue-eyed blonde, a rebel from the start!
My world became perfect, a sister to love with all my heart.
The years that followed challenged us, too many ways
to describe.
But we've held strong, forever friends, always side by side.

Making our way through adolescence and even a bit beyond.
Forbidden questions we unraveled—or so at least we thought.
Eventually, a different path and new friendships came to be.
Sadness still lingers at the loss—"growing-up" time is hard
to leave.

You were the conservative Catholic, such a legacy of
family commitment.
I talked you into trouble—making sense of each predicament!
You stood by me through many struggles; when I couldn't
make myself be heard.
That love and kind allegiance dear friend, from you I learned.

So many firsts you and I, life and love in our late teens.
We had the magic of our youth and the planning of
our dreams.
But the future we designed wasn't meant to be,
God set His sights beyond the realm, our eyes just couldn't see.

Destination changed direction; so many twists and turns along
the way.
You rescued my soul, restored, redeemed, bringing hope that
wondrous day.
Never could I imagine the blessings forward, from following
Your lead,
My Continued Constant and Creator, my Lord and
Eternal King.

With trust and apprehension I prayed, "God bring my soul
mate to fruition."
More than I could ask for, he's my best friend. Your perfect
selection.

When the memory of broken generations brought with it
doubt and tears,
His calming words "we'll break the chain," brought freedom
from those fears.

I write these words to honor you, with humble,
heartfelt emotion,
Thank you dear friends for loyalty, sweet love and
kind devotion.
Your presence throughout my life and the memories I hold
so dear,
Though time or distance may intrude, in my heart you're
forever near.
—*Teresa Alley*

Soul Food

"For I know the plans I have for you," declares the LORD, "plans to prosper you and not to harm you, plans to give you hope and a future. Then you will call upon me and come and pray to me, and I will listen to you."

(JEREMIAH 29:11-12)

Personal Reflection Or Group Discussion

1. Take a trip down memory lane. Describe your first best friend? What is it that drew you to her/him. Are you still in contact?

2. As we grow older and experience life, we change. What has that looked like with different friendships—positive or negative?

3. What do you hold most precious in your friendships and why?

About the Author

TERESA ALLEY was born and raised in Washington State and moved to Colorado in 1978. There she met her husband and they began a life journey, the best of which was raising their three children. Currently, they are experiencing the blessing of being Nana and Pops to their three precious grandchildren. Teresa's greatest joy is spending time with family, friends, and their Australian Labradoodle, Max.

Eclectic Encouragement is her first nonfiction book.

CPSIA information can be obtained
at www.ICGtesting.com
Printed in the USA
LVHW030024210720
661166LV00004B/1061